ADAPTING TO FLOODING AND RISING SEA LEVELS

To Carolyn Meyer, the most eco-friendly person I know

Published in 2013 by The Rosen Publishing Group, Inc.
29 East 21st Street, New York, NY 10010

Library of Congress Cataloging-in-Publication Data

Meyer, Susan, 1986–
Adapting to flooding and rising sea levels/Susan Meyer. — 1st ed.
    p. cm. — (Science to the rescue: Adapting to climate change.)
Includes bibliographical references and index.
ISBN 978-1-4488-6847-6 (library binding)
1. Sea level — Climatic factors. 2. Floods. 3. Climatic changes. I. Title.
GC89.M49 2012
363.34'936 — dc23

                                                                2011045624

Manufactured in the United States of America

CPSIA Compliance Information: Batch #S12YA: For further information, contact Rosen Publishing, New York, New York, at 1-800-237-9932.

On the cover: A home and the roads and land that surround it are swamped by rising floodwaters. This kind of flooding will become more common and devastating with global warming and the rising sea levels and increasingly frequent and intense storminess associated with it.

CONtents

INTROduction

With a population of over eight million people, New York City is the largest urban center in the United States. Even if you haven't been to the Big Apple yourself, you have likely seen it countless times in movies and television shows, and you can probably picture many of its iconic landmarks. From the sky-scraping Empire State Building to the bright lights of Times Square and the fast-paced wheeling and dealing of Wall Street, it is a city that exudes speed, power, money, and a long-standing history. Now that you have pictured this world famous city, imagine that it is in grave and imminent danger from a threat that scientists have been studying for a while and are currently trying to better understand.

New York City, along with many other major American and international cities that are situated along coastlines, is in danger because of rising sea levels. For many years, the world's oceans have been slowly rising because of factors related to global warming. In the following chapters, we will discuss some of the reasons global warming causes sea levels to rise. One of the dangerous effects of a rise in ocean levels is that seawater can surge into coastal cities, leading to devastating flooding and catastrophic water damage. The northeastern coast of the United States is among the world's most vulnerable regions to a significant rise in sea levels.

Although scientists disagree on the exact numbers and no one can predict it with any certainty, by 2100 the global sea level is expected to rise between 10–12 inches (250–300 millimeters). Because of the unique position of New York City on the northeast coast and the ocean currents there, the sea level rise around New York City is expected to be at least an additional 8 inches (200 mm) above the global average. The most densely populated of New York City's five boroughs is the island of Manhattan, which is less than 16 feet (4.8 meters) above sea level. Parts of Lower Manhattan,

A man walks along a flooded seawall in downtown Manhattan during Hurricane Irene's landfall in August 2011. Big storms like Irene present a very real threat to New York City. This threat is increased by rising sea levels.

where Wall Street and the financial district are located, are only around 5 feet (1.5 m) above sea level. That means that as sea levels rise, New York is in increasing danger, especially if a hurricane or winter storm surge occurs. Much of this legendary city could be destroyed.

In August 2011, this looming threat became far less abstract and speculative. A hint of things to come arrived in a powerful dose of high-impact reality: Hurricane Irene. This Category 2 storm menaced the city, causing three hundred thousand people to be evacuated and the city's famed subway system to be shut down for over twenty-four hours. Although the storm spared New York City for the most part, it caused devastating flooding in Pennsylvania, New Jersey, Connecticut, and Vermont. Hurricanes and large tropical storms are inevitable, and next time, New York may not be so lucky.

New York City isn't the only major city with a large population living in danger of rising sea levels. Currently, there are 643 million people around the world living in low-lying coastal areas that are at risk for climate change–related flooding. Two-thirds of the world's cities with populations of over five million are on this list, from Los Angeles, California, to Rio de Janeiro in Brazil and Sydney in Australia. Additionally, over half of the total population of the continent of Asia lives in these at-risk, low-lying areas.

Knowing all that we stand to lose—from major cities to coastline habitats—it is extremely important that we start looking at ways to slow down or combat global warming and the related, highly destructive and deadly consequences of rising ocean levels now. This book outlines much of the current research being done to help nations and communities adapt to these new challenges, including new flood-control infrastructures and technologies. It also investigates efforts to slow the process of global warming and reveals the things you as an individual, community member, and citizen of the world can do to help reverse the everyday habits and practices that have resulted in global climate change. For it is our own actions that are endangering not only our fragile planet but human life itself.

CHAPTER one
The Truth About Rising Sea Levels

Throughout Earth's long history, the levels of the oceans have risen and fallen over time. What is sea level exactly? Sea level is defined as the measurement of the level of seawater, after averaging out short-term variations due to wind and waves. In the short term, the sea level rises and falls due to perfectly normal phenomena like tides and strong winds. Over the long term, however, the global sea level has changed at different points in Earth's history. These widespread, long-term changes to Earth's sea levels are known

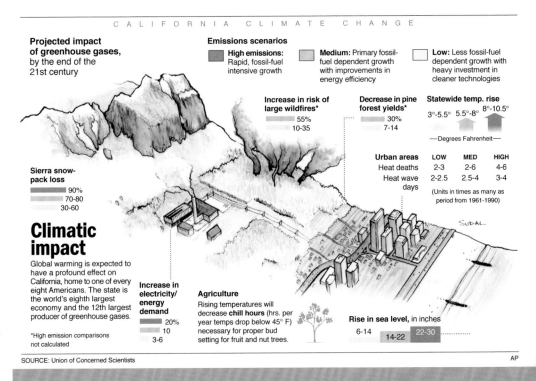

CALIFORNIA CLIMATE CHANGE

Projected impact of greenhouse gases, by the end of the 21st century

Emissions scenarios

- **High emissions:** Rapid, fossil-fuel intensive growth
- **Medium:** Primary fossil-fuel dependent growth with improvements in energy efficiency
- **Low:** Less fossil-fuel dependent growth with heavy investment in cleaner technologies

Increase in risk of large wildfires*
- 55%
- 10-35

Decrease in pine forest yields*
- 30%
- 7-14

Statewide temp. rise
3°-5.5°   5.5°-8°   8°-10.5°

—Degrees Fahrenheit—

Urban areas	LOW	MED	HIGH
Heat deaths	2-3	2-6	4-6
Heat wave days	2-2.5	2.5-4	3-4

(Units in times as many as period from 1961-1990)

Sierra snow-pack loss
- 90%
- 70-80
- 30-60

Climatic impact

Global warming is expected to have a profound effect on California, home to one of every eight Americans. The state is the world's eighth largest economy and the 12th largest producer of greenhouse gases.

*High emission comparisons not calculated

Increase in electricity/ energy demand
- 20%
- 10
- 3-6

Agriculture
Rising temperatures will decrease **chill hours** (hrs. per year temps drop below 45° F) necessary for proper bud setting for fruit and nut trees.

Rise in sea level, in inches
6-14   14-22   22-30

SOURCE: Union of Concerned Scientists

AP

This graphic shows some of the projected consequences of greenhouse gas emissions that are likely to occur in the twenty-first century. Although the drawing specifically refers to California coastlines, many similar effects will be felt in coastal areas around the world.

as eustatic changes. Eustatic changes can cause the overall level of the oceans to rise or fall based on outside forces. These outside forces can include water being added to the oceans because of melting from glaciers and ice sheets, as well as a process called thermal expansion, which will be discussed later in this chapter.

Scientists now believe that many of these outside forces that are raising sea levels worldwide are the direct result of global warming caused by human activity. Most of the energy people use every day to drive their cars, power their homes, and run their factories and businesses comes from the burning of carbon-based fossil fuels. This produces gases that become trapped in Earth's atmosphere. These emissions are called greenhouse gases because, like a greenhouse trapping the sunlight's heat, carbon emissions build up in the atmosphere and prevent heat from escaping. The accumulation of greenhouse gases in the atmosphere and the resulting buildup of heat causes Earth's overall temperature to rise over time. When the air around Earth heats up, water temperatures also rise. When water is warmed it expands, so the result of warmer ocean waters is a rise in sea levels.

Over the course of the twentieth century, overall sea levels have risen on average .08 inches (2 mm) every year. This might not sound like very much. How could anyone notice a rise of just a fraction of an inch? But that added up to about 8 inches (203 mm) by the end of the twentieth century. Like a snowball rolling down a hill, over the course of a century, these little variations add up to much bigger changes. The total rise in sea level during the twenty-first century is estimated to be anywhere from 9.8 inches (25 centimeters) to as much as 20 inches (50.8 cm).

WHY ARE SEA LEVELS RISING?

According to scientists who study climate change, there are two main reasons that the sea levels are rising in response to higher global temperatures. The first reason is because of ice melting from glaciers, ice sheets, and other large masses of ice around the world. Currently, glaciers and ice sheets cover about 10 percent of the world's total land area. These slow moving masses of ice cover parts of every continent except Australia. They are made up of freshwater that was frozen long ago during the last ice age.

These masses of ice hold approximately 75 percent of the world's supply of freshwater. This means that all the freshwater that fills Earth's lakes and rivers, the water that rains from the sky, and the water that people use from their faucets all over the world, every day, accounts for only a quarter of Earth's total supply of freshwater. The rest is locked up in the form of ice.

These small icebergs have broken off from the San Rafael Glacier in Chile. Due largely to the effects of global warming, this enormous glacier is retreating by about 330 feet (100 meters) a year.

Ice is just water transformed into a solid state due to sub-freezing temperatures. When the temperature rises, therefore, ice melts and assumes a liquid state. The higher the temperature rises, the faster large ice sheets melt. Over the past century, many of the glaciers and ice sheets in both Greenland and Antarctica have lost mass. Their mass is the total measure of what they are composed of. The ice sheets and glaciers lose mass when the mass balance is negative. The mass balance is the difference between the amount of ice that is added in the winter and the amount of ice that melts away in the summer. So a negative mass balance means that more ice is melting than is being added during the colder months. The glaciers lose their overall mass and grow smaller as their meltwater enters the ocean.

The world's two largest ice sheets are the Greenland Ice Sheet in the northern hemisphere and the East and West Antarctic Sheets in the southern hemisphere. For scientists to understand how quickly ocean levels may rise and how extensive the problem of melting ice is, they must study these ice sheets as well as smaller glaciers to see how quickly they are changing. It is important that they study both how much ice is melting and its rate of melt (how quickly it is happening).

THERMAL EXPANSION

Glacial melting accounts for a large part of rising sea levels, but there is another major contributor to the phenomenon. The rising temperature of our Earth over time causes the existing ocean water to actually expand. How is this possible? It's actually a very simple law of physics called thermal expansion. Thermal expansion means that liquids increase in volume when they are heated. This means that the same amount of seawater will take up more space if it grows warmer.

FLOODING IN JAPAN

It can be hard to visualize how a few feet of water can become so catastrophic. However, the threat is very real. Many communities will become more vulnerable to storm surges that are the direct result of hurricanes, tropical storms, and tsunamis.

This unfortunate possibility became a tragic reality for Japan in March 2011, when a very powerful earthquake occurred underwater approximately 40 miles (64 kilometers) east of the island nation. This earthquake caused a giant tsunami, with waves over 100 feet (30 m) high and storm surges that traveled up to 6 miles (10 km) inland. The storm surges were so powerful that one of Japan's islands, Honshu, was moved 8 feet (2.5 m) eastward. The ensuing flood resulted in over 15,000 deaths, while hundreds of thousands of residents were forced to flee their homes. Additionally, over 125,000 buildings were damaged or destroyed. A nuclear meltdown at a flooded power plant added to the already unimaginable devastation and panic.

This was the kind of enormous tragedy that, sadly, may become more frequent as sea levels rise around the globe. Powerful storms and natural disasters like the one that wreaked havoc in Japan are already inevitable, but rising ocean waters make them that much more deadly.

To understand why this happens, you must understand the three states of matter. Water can exist in the world as a solid, a liquid, and a gas. When it is a gas—water vapor—it takes up much more space than when it is a liquid. When water is heated to its boiling point and becomes water vapor, it means that the molecules in water are moving farther and farther apart and taking up more space. The temperatures of the ocean waters are nowhere near boiling point, but they are getting warmer, so the water molecules are slowly moving farther apart. The result is a greater volume of water that causes the overall sea level to rise.

FRAGILE AND THREATENED ECOSYSTEMS

It is not just the people living at the lowest elevations who will be affected. The world also stands to lose important habitats. Wetlands habitats are fragile environments that support many species of plants and animals. Approximately two-thirds of the fish that people eat worldwide depend on coastal wetlands for their survival.

You may think that the rising ocean levels would actually increase wetland habitat by turning existing dry land into wetlands. That is not actually the case, in part because people have built cities and walls along many of the coasts to prevent coastal encroachment. These urban and highly developed areas would not be able to sustain life if flooded. If water temperatures and sea levels rise as much as expected, there

Arctic animals, such as this polar bear, depend on snow and ice for their survival. In 2008, polar bears were added to the list of threatened species under the Endangered Species Act.

will also be loss of habitat in Arctic and Antarctic regions. Polar bears and other wildlife depend for their survival upon the ice that is now melting.

Another problem posed by rising sea levels is increased salinity (saltiness) in the world's freshwater sources. There is a limited amount of freshwater on Earth, and this water is vital to all plant, animal, and human life. Humans cannot live for very long at all without water, and neither can plants and other animals. As salt water from the oceans rises and moves inland, it could flood rivers and freshwater reservoirs, contaminating the water we need to stay alive.

Given the vast number of negative consequences that will result directly or indirectly from rising ocean levels and flooding, these is a strong need for the development of flood prevention and response strategies and technologies. Luckily, scientists and government organizations around the globe are looking at ways to help solve these grave challenges.

CHAPTER two

Responding to the Threat

Imagine if we could predict the future—if the stock market would go up or down, who would win a war between two countries, or the exact place and time in which an earthquake would occur. If we could accurately predict any of these events, it would be worth billions of dollars and, in some cases, save many lives. The same is true of predicting the results of a rise in sea levels. For this reason, like the army of men in suits who attempt to predict the mysterious workings of the stock market every day, there is an army of scientists and government agencies working tirelessly to combat the global effects of rising sea levels. They are also attempting to determine exactly how the rising tides will affect coastal communities and surrounding plant, animal, and human life.

A LONG-RANGE CRISIS

People have had to deal with changing sea levels for thousands of years. Some of the earliest humans dealt with rising sea levels after the last ice age simply by moving inland. However, these early humans did not have the same technologies and concerns that people have today. Today, our coasts are lined with large cities and expensive beachfront housing. The time has come for people to start looking for solutions to changing coastlines, the huge impact rising sea levels will have on them, and the challenges of relocating or effectively protecting coastal communities.

As part of this research, scientists are looking at ways that global warming—the trigger for rising sea levels— can be slowed down. Unfortunately, global warming has already had a major impact upon the world's oceans. Reversing those negative effects will be extremely difficult and require a long period of time. It is still imperative that scientists and everyday people continue working to slow down the warming process, but a degree of damage has already been done to the oceans even though we can't always see it with the naked eye. This is due to the process called thermal inertia.

Thermal inertia means that the warming observed in the oceans appears later than the comparable changes we see in air temperature. If you've ever jumped headfirst into a

Miami is the second-largest city in Florida, with a population of nearly 400,000 people. However, as can be seen in this photo, it is also a city at high risk for flooding based on its position directly on the Atlantic coastline.

swimming pool, lake, or ocean in early summer, you know that even when the air is starting to get very hot, the water may still be cool for another few weeks. This is because of thermal inertia. Water warms more slowly than air, but it also holds on to the accumulated and stored heat long after the air has again cooled. So, even if global warming can be slowed or reversed, the oceans will continue to remain warmer than normal for a considerable period of time. As a result, the threat of higher sea levels and flooding will continue even if carbon emissions are slashed and global warming is somehow brought under control. It is therefore very important for scientists to come up with solutions to the threats posed by rising sea levels that, to some degree, are now inevitable.

UNDER THE ICE

On a map and in photographs, Antarctica might appear to be one massive island of ice, but there is actually a great mass of earth under much of it. In the eastern part of Antarctica, there is a continent the size of Australia under the enormous, often mile-thick (1.6 km) ice sheet. If the ice sheet on top of East Antarctica were to melt in its entirety, it would raise the global sea level by a whopping 197 feet (60 m). As the global climate rises, this ice shelf is slowly melting.

West Antarctica is different from East Antarctica. Whereas East Antarctica is composed of a large ice sheet covering a vast and continuous expanse of earth, West Antarctica's ice sheet covers a series of smaller islands. Parts of the West Antarctica Ice Sheet (or WAIS) are actually attached to the ocean floor, not to land. If the WAIS were to melt, it would raise the global sea level by 16 to 23 feet (5 to 7 meters). Because so much of the ice sheet is in contact with the ocean rather than with land, West Antarctica is in greater danger of melting due to increased ocean temperatures.

Much of West Antarctica is indeed melting away from underneath. There is no way to monitor this melting with the help of satellites because it happens below the surface of Earth's oceans. When an accurate picture is finally gained, it may be too late to do anything about it.

THE THREE RESPONSES

There are a number of different ways humans can adapt to the challenges posed by rising sea levels. Most of these different methods of adaptation can be divided into three main categories: retreat, accommodation, and protection. Retreat is exactly what it sounds like—moving inland rather than making an attempt to stop ocean waters from encroaching on land. With a retreat strategy, the coastal zone is abandoned and all ecosystems shift inland if possible. This choice might be made in places where trying to do anything else would come at great environmental or economic cost.

The second option is accommodation. Accommodation means accepting that sea levels will rise and salt water will move inland. Allowances are made for these changes. The coastal area is allowed to be flooded, and the area's life-forms, including humans, attempt to coexist with the changes to the environment. This option includes measures like elevating buildings on piles so they can withstand floods, converting agricultural areas to fish farming or salt tolerant crops, and erecting emergency flood shelters in anticipation of storm surges.

Finally, one of the most frequently employed adaptive strategies is protection. Protection means using physical barriers to prevent sea levels from encroaching on communities; existing buildings, homes, and infrastructure; and freshwater sources. These protective structures might include sea walls and dikes, but also more natural flood-control solutions like the stabilizing of dunes and vegetation in coastal areas.

This photo shows the harbor in the city of Bremerhaven, in Germany. Rising sea levels have required increased spending to create new infrastructure to protect this important port.

The appropriate response to rising sea levels depends largely on the economic and natural resources of the area in question. Different responses make sense for different environments and localities. The implementation of these three main response types will also vary. If land for new settlement is available inland, retreat can be implemented by local, state, or national governments. The government can revise land use regulations and change building codes so that people will no longer be able to build certain structures in at-risk areas. They will then have no choice but to build the structures they want in safer inland areas. Accommodation can be implemented, not with government action, but through the innovations of scientists, architects, and inventors. Protection can be implemented mostly by the government authorities who are responsible for overseeing and guaranteeing water resources and coastal protection.

In addition to the retreat, accommodation, and protection strategies, a primary goal for scientists and government agencies, like the Environmental Protection Agency (EPA), is

Water rushes through the floodgates of a Sri Lankan dam. Sri Lanka is an island nation off the coast of India long threatened by flooding from large storms called monsoons. The danger has only increased with rising sea levels.

to increase knowledge and awareness of the problem and the dangers it poses. This is a critical component of any response strategy they undertake. Alternatively, the most important goal of any climate research agency is to create the most accurate projections possible for the likely rate of sea level increase. This important aspect of research will help all those tasked with preparing for and coping with rising ocean levels to determine which of the three strategies—retreat, accommodation, or protection—or which combination of them, is warranted in each particular situation.

CHAPTER three

Real-World Solutions to Rising Sea Levels

n the previous chapter we looked at some of the ways that people can respond to the impact of rising sea levels resulting from global climate change. Now we can focus on some of the real-world applications of these different responses, both in the United States and in countries all over the world. We will look at several specific cases of communities adapting to rising sea levels to illustrate the different types of responses—retreat, accommodation, and protection.

RETREAT BY NECESSITY IN BANGLADESH

One of the world's most heavily populated areas that is in danger of flooding because of rising sea levels is the country of Bangladesh, a small nation that borders India. Bangladesh has a large coastline, and two rivers flow through its fertile plains where most of the nation's food is grown. These rivers, the Ganges and the Meghna, have large flood plains that, due to rising ocean levels, could effectively wipe out much of the nation's agriculture. Salty floodwaters would destroy crops and ruin soil. In addition, as many as thirty million people could be displaced by the floodwaters, and iconic animal species like the Bengal tiger could be lost.

The threat to Bangladesh of global warming–induced rising floodwaters is a disaster waiting to happen for the nation's impoverished population. The country is frequently battered by tropical storms and tornadoes, which funnel along its coast and cause great destruction across the low-lying delta. As a result, the country is accustomed to regular floods. Yet the flooding is now expected to become both more frequent and more catastrophic. Sea levels along the coast are rising fast, as are water temperatures, making Bangladesh one of the most heavily populated areas in the world so highly vulnerable to the effects of climate change.

In Bangladesh, people in coastal areas are moving whole villages inland by carrying all their possessions on their backs, as their towns flood and their agriculture is threatened. In this poverty-stricken country, retreat is the only feasible option.

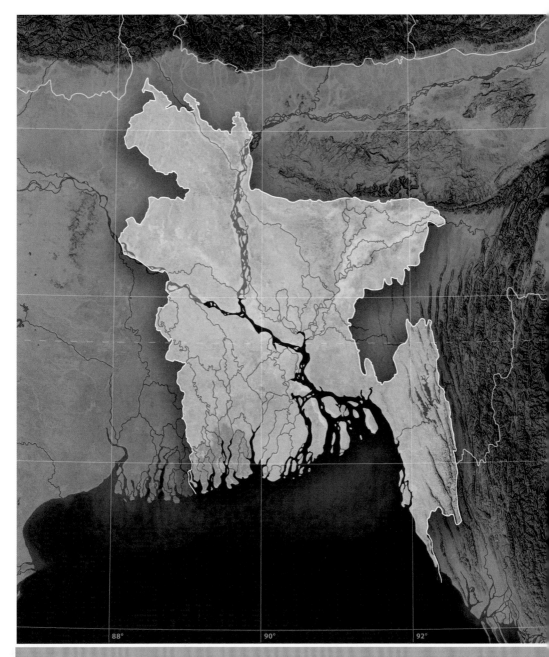

A topographic map shows the country of Bangladesh, situated on the southern coast of the Asian continent. Rising sea levels have caused devastating losses for the agriculturally dependent nation as floods destroy its crops and coastal towns. The nation's swollen rivers are clearly seen in dark blue.

ACCOMMODATION THROUGH SALTWATER FARMING

Not everyone is prepared or able to retreat from coastal areas. Some scientists and researchers are looking for ways in which agricultural land can still be used even after it is flooded with seawater. Atmospheric physicist Carl Hodges started the Seawater Foundation to study methods for accommodating higher ocean levels. Rather than preventing seawater from flooding land, Hodges believes that flooded land can be used for agricultural purposes.

The plan is to cut channels through the land to draw seawater inland where the salt water can be used. This prevents the water from building up along the coast and forcing its way into cities and coastal farms where soil and crops will be destroyed by salty water. By drawing seawater away from these areas and toward places ready and able to accommodate the water, it will help to protect the most flood-sensitive and threatened areas.

In many cases, these seawater channels will be used to irrigate coastal deserts. The channels will not only help lower rising sea levels, but they will also turn these barren regions into potentially productive aquafarms. What sort of farm could use salt water to help things grow? These are questions that the Global Seawater Foundation and other organizations and researchers are beginning to investigate more closely. Currently, aquafarms could be used to raise shrimp, fish, and other seafood. There are also certain plants, like forms of edible seaweed, that can thrive in salt water.

The Seawater Foundation (www.seawaterfoundation.org) is a nonprofit organization dedicated to creating sustainable communities and agriculture in Earth's coastal deserts. Its work is very important for adapting to rising sea levels and the loss of coastlines worldwide.

These could be grown in aquafarms and help to feed nearby communities and fertilize surrounding agricultural areas.

The mission of the Seawater Foundation has been successful in the east African nation of Eritrea. A seawater irrigation channel system has provided jobs for 800 people, cultivated 100 acres (404,686 sq. meters) of seawater-tolerant crops, and produced enough excess shrimp to export to other nations. This is no small feat in a country that has long been susceptible to poverty and famine.

MAINE RETREATS AND ACCOMMODATES

The government of the state of Maine has begun to take steps to limit development in coastal areas that have been considered at risk for flooding. This includes putting restrictions on the number and type of houses that can be built in these areas. For example, only houses that are structurally able to withstand up to a 10-foot (3 m) rise in ocean levels can be built in these coastal areas. This means that people who can't build such structures are being forced to build their houses or businesses inland.

This is a form of retreat response because it involves people moving away from affected areas as a solution. Yet it also reflects the accommodation strategy, in that houses specifically engineered to withstand floods can still be built in the threatened coastal areas. While Maine's coastal residents might spend a greater amount to build flood-resistant houses or retreat inland, they will be happy they did when sea levels rise and their homes are either prepared to weather the storm waters or are situated safely away from the flood-prone coast.

PROTECTING CITIES WITH STRONG BARRIERS

One example of how researchers and engineers have used the protection method of flood prevention is in the safeguarding of one of the largest cities in the world: London, England. In 1982, a barrier was built across the Thames River. The

The Thames flood barrier includes enormous floodgates that can be opened to allow boats to pass along the river. The barrier on the Thames is the second-largest moveable floodgate in the world, after the Oosterscheldekering in the Netherlands.

Thames is the river that runs directly through the center of London. The barrier is one of the largest movable flood barriers in the world. It spans 1,706 feet (520 m) across the river. It has ten steel gates that can be raised into position across the river. These gates are kept open most of the time to allow ships to travel through this important waterway. However, the Thames Barrier can be closed at any time if the city is threatened by rising waters and flooding. When closed, each gate is as tall as a five-story building.

Another example of protection can be found in the Netherlands. The Netherlands is a small country in central Europe. It is one of the so-called Low Countries (along with Belgium, Luxembourg, and parts of northern France and western Germany), a territory situated in the low-lying delta of the Rhine, Scheldt, and Meuse rivers. The use of the term "low" is apt, for half of the Netherlands lies less than 3 feet (1 m) above sea level, and one-quarter of the country actually sits below sea level.

The Netherlands has a sophisticated system of dikes, dams, and storm barriers to prevent flooding, but it remains very vulnerable to the destructive effects of rising sea levels. In many ways, the Netherlands has already done all it can within its own borders to prevent storm surges and catastrophic flooding. To further protect itself, the country will need to look beyond its borders.

The Netherlands can join forces with neighboring European countries that share a coastline along a body of water called the North Sea to create a cooperative coastal management system. This would include such things as manipulating sediment deposits in the North Sea to slow the sea level's rise and perhaps even exert some measure of control over it. Another example of what this group might accomplish is widening riverbanks inland to create more places for water to be contained safely without flooding cities, towns, and farms.

CHAPTER four

Adapting to the Future

As you learn more about the ways that scientists and lawmakers are helping people adapt to the effects of global climate change, you see that there are a lot of different flood-control strategies currently being put into practice all around the globe. Scientists and government officials recognize the need to spend money and resources now in order to prevent greater economic, environmental, and human loss in the future.

While there are a number of clever strategies currently being deployed worldwide, there are also a number of ideas that are still on the drawing board or in the research phase. All of these cutting-edge, "next generation" ideas should be considered carefully as we continue to confront future environmental challenges and plan for the worst.

USING TECHNOLOGY TO IMPROVE PREDICTIONS

One of the major problems with figuring out how to adapt to climate change is that we don't currently have a precise sense of how high global sea levels will rise. Scientists can make theoretical projections and educated guesses based on what they know of thermal expansion and the rate of global melting. Yet they often provide fairly wide ranges, such as the oft-cited prediction of a 0.6 to 2 feet (0.18 to 0.61 m) rise in sea levels over the next century. This is because it's hard to predict, much less fully understand, the natural processes at work, and therefore impossible to cite exact numbers. This makes it difficult to effectively prepare for a problem that we don't grasp the true extent of yet.

A recent research study in Australia conducted by the Wealth from Oceans National Research Flagship seeks to clear up this uncertainty and draw definitive conclusions that can lead to direct and concrete action. It is using computer models to figure out the exact impact that erosion and flooding will have on Australian beaches. The group's sea level research is focused on understanding the past to better predict the future.

Australian researchers are working to combat rising flood tides by studying tidal patterns and sea level changes on their beaches. This photo shows the destruction wrought on Australia's Mission Beach by a large storm and ocean surge.

The Flagship is studying relatively recent sea level changes from the twentieth and twenty-first centuries and using this data as a basis for improving projections of future rises in sea level. Flagship researchers gather data from instruments that measure the tides, but they also use sophisticated equipment like satellite altimeters. A satellite altimeter is an orbiting satellite that is used to measure past changes in global and regional mean sea level. Most important, the researchers attempt to understand the processes at work in these past sea level fluctuations. By understanding what may have triggered past rises in sea level, and the extent of those increases, the researchers hope to arrive at a far more detailed and accurate assessment of what is currently being experienced and what can be expected in the years ahead.

All of this will allow for better decision making, preparation, and emergency response as sea levels rise. In addition, the Flagship's research could be applied, potentially, not only to Australia's beaches but to other wetland and coastal habitats as well. By better understanding the problem and its potential extent before it arrives, communities will be able to prepare for and adapt to the changing conditions far more quickly, efficiently, and effectively. A more informed and efficient response to rising sea levels will save money, time, and, quite possibly, many human lives.

RETREAT, ACCOMMODATION, OR PROTECTION: THE FUTURE OF NEW YORK CITY

In the introduction, the dangers posed to New York City in the event of a large storm surge were outlined. Lower Manhattan, parts of which are only a few feet above sea level, is particularly vulnerable to flooding and global warming–related rises in ocean levels. Some of the current plans being considered for the future of New York City reveal the range of possible response strategies.

A city of canals, Venice frequently faces challenges from what its citizens call *acqua alta,* or "high water." In recent years, the city has seen more and more instances of these rising waters destroying the city's beautiful buildings and irreplaceable relics.

A number of urban planners have been taxed with the job of coming up with solutions. One Columbia University research scientist, Klaus Jacob, believes the response to the increased likelihood of urban flooding should be a combination of retreat and accommodation. He suggests the sea level rise may force some New Yorkers to pull back from low-lying areas. City authorities will then have to make the areas on higher ground more densely populated. They could then turn the flood-prone areas into parks and other buffer zones between the surging water and residential and commercial buildings.

According to Jacob's vision, New York City in two hundred years may come to resemble the Italian city of Venice. Venice is famous for being filled with canals that people can use to get from place to place. These canals go between the buildings like streets do in a regular city. If Jacob's proposed ideas are adopted, in the years before the ocean rises enough to spill into Manhattan, dozens of skyscrapers in Lower Manhattan will have been protected in advance. Jacob proposes sealing the base of threatened buildings and adding new entrances to higher floors. The streets of the financial district, including the iconic Wall Street, will become canals. In this vision, which is essentially an accommodation strategy, people could take boats to get from place to place and still use the existing buildings. Many scientists are not comfortable with this type of scenario, however, because it would still require the moving of thousands of people to higher and safer ground. These are people who have, in some cases, lived in these neighborhoods for generations.

Another projected solution for New York City's potential flooding problems pursues a protection strategy. One oceanographer (a scientist who studies oceans) named Malcolm Bowman believes a possible solution is to build a wall to protect the city from storm surges. This would not be just any wall though. This barrier would extend from the East River to the Long Island Sound, an area of nearly 2 miles (3 km). The structures at their highest points would be 30 feet (9 m) above the harbor surface. Like the barriers that protect the city of London on the Thames, these barriers would be open most of the time to let ships pass through to the city's waterways. They would only be closed when hurricanes or other severe storms threatened the city.

Preliminary engineering studies put the cost of this project at around $11 billion. Yet the time for many at-risk cities like New York to start considering seemingly radical and even costly solutions is now. The costs of the effects of a catastrophic disaster are always higher than preparations for one. And tomorrow may already be too late.

ARCHITECTURE FOR THE FUTURE

As scientists research ways to adapt to the effects of climate change and rising sea levels, architects and designers are also investigating and testing ways to help the world adapt. They are seeking to create new urban infrastructure and systems that will be able to withstand future climate changes.

Given what we learned about the Netherlands' proximity to sea level in chapter 3, it's no wonder the Dutch are at the forefront of designing innovative and flood-resistant housing. A Dutch construction company believes that the solution is to build amphibious houses as extensions of cities currently situated in flood plains. It contends that floating houses could minimize the amount of land and housing lost to flooding.

These new Dutch houses, which are part of a development program called the Maasbommel Project, are built of timber and concrete. Their foundations will be composed of a series of hollow concrete pontoons. The pontoons will be able to rise when floodwaters come, and the homes will

These floating houses are part of the Maasbommel Project in the Netherlands. They can rise and fall with the water level and represent a method of accommodating rising sea levels by building structures that can coexist with flooding.

remain dry and buoyant. The houses' main structure, meanwhile, is light and similar to a boat. Each house will contain flexible pipes and ducts that will ensure that water will run, toilets will flush, and lights can be turned on and off just like in any house, even during a flood. Boats can be parked alongside the houses just like cars.

The houses are currently projected to be too expensive for the average Dutch citizen to be able to afford. The company points out, however, that the cost of building flood-proof houses and offices is less than the amount of money the government currently spends on constructing and operating flood barriers. The Maasbommel Project has big plans for the future. The company wants to one day build a town of twelve thousand homes, which could include everything from houses and stores to schools and even hospitals.

NEXT GENERATION ARK

Every year, the Union of Architects sponsors a contest all over the world called Architecture for Disaster Relief. Architects submit designs they think will help solve world problems and large-scale disasters. One of these submissions was specifically designed to make expanding human habitation on and near oceans possible. The design is for a hotel concept called Ark. Ark can be built on land, or in the event of the loss of some land to floodwaters, it can be constructed as a floating building.

The design includes a greenhouse to grow fresh food, and the structure is designed to collect and store rainwater. Ark is powered by a combination of wind and thermal energy derived from both the air and water. For this reason, it is well suited to weather some of the worst effects of global warming while creating a very small carbon footprint.

Ark might look like a futuristic design, and it may never be built, but it illustrates how architects are committed to coming up with unique solutions to real-world problems.

GEOENGINEERING: ACTIVELY CHANGING OUR CLIMATE

Some ideas for adapting to the negative effects of climate change are more feasible than others. Some scientists and mechanical engineers think we can halt rising sea levels by reversing climate change. We can do this not by reducing our carbon-based energy use but by taking direct action to engineer our climate to best suit the needs of life on Earth. The process they suggest is commonly known as geoengineering.

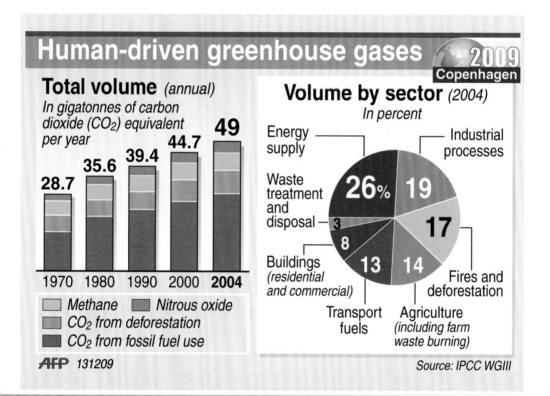

This chart shows the major human contributions to the greenhouse gases that build up in our atmosphere and cause global temperatures to rise. It breaks down the human activities that are most directly responsible for global warming and rising sea levels.

The National Academy of Science defines geoengineering as a large-scale changing of our environment in order to combat the effects of changes in atmospheric chemistry. It is fair to say we are already geoengineering our world by changing the environment—for the worse—through the emission of greenhouse gases. Therefore, some people think a solution is to try to reverse these negative warming-related changes to the environment with further human intervention. Their philosophy can be summed up as follow: we caused the problem, we should also be able to fix it.

But how does geoengineering work? We know we have the power to change our climate for the worse, but do we also have the power to improve it? The most common theory of geoengineering involves compensating for the rise in global temperatures (caused by an increase in greenhouse gases) by reflecting or scattering back a fraction of the incoming sunlight, so it escapes the atmosphere instead of getting trapped in it.

Another geoengineering possibility is to reforest the United States to increase the storage of carbon in plants. Trees and plants absorb carbon dioxide as part of their normal respiration cycles. In fact, forests are considered a "carbon sink" because of their ability to absorb enormous quantities of carbon, removing it from the atmosphere. By decreasing the amount of carbon in the atmosphere, the amount of excess heat that is trapped there will also decrease. Another way to decrease carbon in the atmosphere through geoengineering is by stimulating the growth of living plants and carbon-eating bacteria in the ocean as a means of increasing the natural storage of carbon there. Oceans, like forests, are considered an important and effective carbon sink.

All of these methods of geoengineering have one thing in common. They don't aim to reduce energy usage and carbon emissions. Rather, they all involve capturing and storing greenhouse gases so they cannot enter or linger in Earth's atmosphere. Many scientists are skeptical and wary of these large-scale, aggressive attempts to alter our climate because these actions may have negative consequences that we cannot yet foresee.

CHAPTER five

Your Impact Upon Rising Sea Levels

Having learned more about the challenges facing the inhabitants of planet Earth because of global warming–related rising sea levels, it can be easy to feel overwhelmed by the situation. While scientists are busy devising and testing exciting new solutions, you may feel helpless to assist. However, there are a lot of things that ordinary individuals can do to help. While scientists predict that some rise in global sea levels is inevitable, there are things you can do in your everyday life to help prevent even more extensive and catastrophic damage in the years ahead. The future of our planet rests in the everyday decisions we make in our daily lives.

Global sea levels are rising for two reasons: thermal expansion and runoff from the increased and accelerating melting of glacial ice. Both of these problems are a result of global warming, which is caused by heat-trapping greenhouse gas emissions building up in our atmosphere. These gases are released into the atmosphere when people burn coal, oil, gasoline, natural gas, and other carbon-based fuels for energy.

Busy cities like Beijing, China (seen here), produce a great deal of pollution that builds up in our atmosphere. Unfortunately, climate-altering greenhouse gases are a by-product of the energy used to run our cars, light our homes, and power our factories.

Driving a car to the grocery store or turning on a light-bulb in your house are minor, everyday activities that require energy. In most cases, this energy is provided by a carbon-based fuel source. Almost every person on the planet uses some type of energy that produces greenhouse gases every day. Everyone is part of the problem, which means anyone and everyone can be part of the solution.

THINGS TO DO IN YOUR EVERYDAY LIFE

Each and every person can help slow and hopefully reverse global climate change. There are a few simple steps that you and your family can take to reduce the amount of energy you use each day. One of the biggest things you can do to avoid increasing the amount of fossil fuels burned and emissions of carbon into the atmosphere is simply to use less energy. There are a number of ways you can do this in your everyday life. First of all, you can make sure to turn off lights and appliances when they are not in use. You should also make sure to unplug electronics like video game consoles, DVD players, DVRs, and cell phone, tablet, and laptop chargers when not in use. Did you know that when they are plugged into the wall, they use energy even when they are not switched on? Turning off and unplugging electronics when they are not in use can save valuable energy every year.

Additionally, not all electronics are created equally. Energy-efficient appliances and electronics typically use between 10 and 50 percent less energy than regular models. While you shouldn't replace appliances that don't yet need to be replaced, if you happen to be shopping for a new

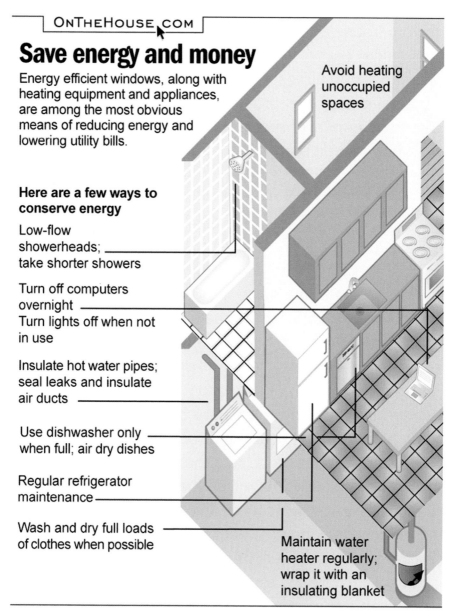

ONTHEHOUSE.COM

Save energy and money

Energy efficient windows, along with heating equipment and appliances, are among the most obvious means of reducing energy and lowering utility bills.

Here are a few ways to conserve energy

Low-flow showerheads; take shorter showers

Turn off computers overnight
Turn lights off when not in use

Insulate hot water pipes; seal leaks and insulate air ducts

Use dishwasher only when full; air dry dishes

Regular refrigerator maintenance

Wash and dry full loads of clothes when possible

Avoid heating unoccupied spaces

Maintain water heater regularly; wrap it with an insulating blanket

Robyn Iris Segal • AP

These are just a few of the many simple ways (from www.onthehouse.com) that you can conserve energy in your home to both save money and help create a brighter future for our planet.

television, computer, refrigerator, washer and dryer, or other electronic device or appliance, take some time to do a little research to find ones that are labeled as energy efficient. Any product with an Energy Star label and certification has met strict government energy efficiency standards.

When you leave your home, you can also make an effort to use less energy when traveling from place to place. If you are in an area where it is safe to walk or ride your bike to get to school or other places you would like to go, try to use these methods of transportation instead of a car. It is also more energy-efficient to take the school bus or other public transportation in your neighborhood than to drive a car. Some places you will still need to drive to, but in those cases, encourage your family to make fewer car trips by combining errands into one big trip instead of several smaller and separate trips. You can also encourage your parents to buy a fuel-efficient hybrid or electric car to further reduce carbon-based emissions.

Another important way you can save energy is by saving water. It takes a lot of energy to treat the water you use every day to make it safe to drink. It takes even more energy to heat the water you use to clean yourself, your clothes, and your dishes. In fact, letting your faucet run with warm water for even five minutes uses about as much energy as it takes to power a sixty-watt lightbulb for a whopping fourteen hours. As you can see, saving water is an important part of saving energy and reducing carbon emissions. You can help to be water-wise by turning off the water while brushing your teeth and making an effort to take shorter showers. You can also talk to your parents about installing water-efficient

Alternative energy sources, like wind and solar energy, are a solution to curbing the amount of greenhouse gases we release into our atmosphere each year. Both wind and solar energy are renewable sources and are ultimately better for our environment.

appliances in your home, such as low-flow plumbing fixtures, toilets, and showerheads. Another way to save water, especially hot water, is to run the dishwasher or washing machine only when it is completely full.

Using less energy is important, but equally important is where your energy comes from. Renewable energy sources like wind and solar power are better for the environment. When we use these sources to power our homes and schools, we avoid the carbon dioxide emissions that would have come from burning coal, oil, or natural gas. You can talk to your parents about switching to a renewable energy source. Perhaps you can install solar panels or a solar water heater or explore green energy options with your local utility provider.

BEACH PATROL

If you live or vacation near the shore, there are steps you can take to cause less damage to the fragile coastal environment. By maintaining the strength and health of coastlines, we make them less likely to erode in the face of rising sea levels. If we don't protect our beaches and coastlines, it will only speed up and intensify the catastrophic effects of rising sea levels and flooding.

One way you can help protect the environment while at the beach is to stay on paths, boardwalks, and designated trails when walking over sand dunes to get to the beach. These pathways are there for a reason. Using them to get to the beach instead of walking across sensitive dunes will help prevent erosion. Dunes protect the land against storm surges from the sea and also provide a home for specialized plants and animals. Human activity can threaten the existence of dunes and make the coastline more susceptible to erosion and flooding.

SAVE THE DUNES!

Many organizations and helpful volunteers are devoted to protecting and maintaining sand dunes on coastlines around the world. One of these groups is the Duxbury Beach Preservation group. It maintains the 6-mile-long (10 km long) Duxbury Beach in southeastern Massachusetts. It is not just adults who contribute to the volunteer effort, but whole families. One member of the group has been bringing her daughter since she was six years old to help teach her about nature and the fragility of the coastal environment. Everyone has the power to help protect dunes.

To combat natural erosion, the Duxbury Beach Preservation group organizes a beach grass planting every spring. American beach grass is planted in tufts by volunteers up and down the dunes. This grass helps hold the dunes together, making them less susceptible to erosion. In the spring of 2011, the group planted over twenty-seven thousand tufts of beach grass. The group also puts up fences to keep people from walking on the dunes and causing damage.

Signs, like this one, warn people to keep from walking on delicate coastal environments. Sand dunes help prevent coastal erosion, which can help slow down the effects of rising sea levels.

People began working to maintain the dunes after a large storm caused great damage to the beach in 1991. Disaster relief experts realized that it was easier and cheaper to repair the beach and keep it strong than to pay for future flood damage inland.

It is also a good idea to go only to beaches that are established for use by people. These include both public and private beaches and state parks. It is not a good idea to visit uninhabited coastline. While it might seem nice to enjoy a deserted and secluded beach, there is probably a reason people are not allowed there. You could be having a negative impact on the health of that coastal environment.

BE THE CHANGE YOU WANT TO SEE IN THE WORLD

The individual can have an impact on his or her environment in a positive way. Part of what you can do is to become educated about carbon emissions, global warming, climate change, rising sea levels, and threats to fragile coastal ecosystems. Then act on what you learn about how to reduce your negative impact on the planet, and tell other people what you know. If everyone learns more about the looming threat of rising sea levels and the ways that people can both fight the threat and adapt to changing conditions, then humanity will be better prepared to face whatever the future brings and greatly increase its chances of survival.

GLOSsary

amphibious Suited for both land and water.

aquafarm An area of salt water used for the production of food.

dike A long wall built to prevent flooding from the sea.

dune A mound or ridge of sand.

encroachment A gradual advance that presents a problem or poses a threat.

eustatic Global changes in sea level.

geoengineering An intentional, large-scale changing of Earth's environment by humans.

glacier A slow moving mass of ice.

greenhouse gas A gas, such as carbon dioxide, that contributes to the greenhouse effect in our atmosphere.

infrastructure Buildings, bridges, tunnels, railways, roads, sewers, electrical grids, telecommunications, and other physical and organizational structures needed for the operation of a society.

mass The quantity of matter that a body contains.

mass balance The amount of mass added to something minus the amount of mass it has lost.

oceanographer A scientist that studies the oceans.

pontoon A hollow metal cylinder used with others of its kind to support a temporary bridge or floating platform.

satellite altimeter An orbiting satellite that is used to measure past changes in global sea level.

sea level The measurement of the level of the seawater after averaging out short-term fluctuations.

sediment Small particles of matter that are carried by wind or water.

storm surge A rising of the sea as a result of a storm and its movement inland from the coast.

thermal expansion The way that matter increases in volume in response to increases in temperature.

thermal inertia Resistance to a change in temperature; a characteristic of water.

tsunami A long, high sea wave, often caused by an earthquake.

volume The amount of space a substance occupies.

wetland An area often covered by shallow water or having soil saturated with water.

FOR MORE INFORmation

Environment Canada
10 Wellington, 23rd floor
Gatineau, QC K1A 0H3
Canada
(819) 997-2800
Web site: http://www.ec.gc.ca
Environment Canada is a department of the Canadian government devoted to protecting the environment and the people of Canada. It has conducted substantial research and presented a number of publications on greenhouse gas emissions, climate change, and the threat of rising sea levels.

Friends of the Earth
1717 Massachusetts Avenue, Suite 600
Washington, DC 20036
(202) 783-7400
Web site: http://www.foe.org
Friends of the Earth and its network of grassroots groups in seventy-seven countries defend the environment and champion a more healthy and just world. Its current campaigns focus on clean energy and solutions to global warming, protecting people from toxic and new, potentially harmful technologies, and promoting smarter, low-pollution transportation alternatives.

Intergovernmental Panel on Climate Change (IPCC)
7bis Avenue de la Paix
C.P. 2300, CH-1211 Geneva 2
Switzerland
Tel.: 41-22-730-8208
Web site: http://www.ipcc.ch

The IPCC is a scientific body created by the United Nations to study and assess the threat posed by climate change. The organization helps the world adapt to the threat of rising sea levels through research on the possible scope of the problem. It also provides public outreach and information on both rising sea levels and climate change in general.

Living Oceans Society
207 West Hastings Street, Suite 1405
Vancouver, BC V6B 1H7
Canada
(250) 973-6580
Web site: http://www.livingoceans.org
The Living Oceans Society is a leader in the effort to protect Canada's coastlines since 1998. It advocates protecting the oceans and coastlines for the good of both humans and animals. Its research into coastal ecosystems and the way that climate change affects the health of these environments is vital to future actions to protect fragile coastlines and adapt to the negative consequences of climate change and rising sea levels.

National Oceanic and Atmospheric Administration (NOAA)
1401 Constitution Avenue NW, Room 5128
Washington, DC 20230
(301) 713-1208
Web site: http://www.noaa.gov
NOAA is a U.S. agency that studies the atmosphere and the oceans. Its mission is to understand and predict environmental changes so we can make the best use of our resources. One of its divisions is the National

Weather Service. Its Web site has tools and information on practically all aspects of climate science and lots of student resources.

Pew Center on Global Climate Change
2101 Wilson Boulevard, Suite 550
Arlingon, VA 22201
(703) 516-4146
Web site: http://www.pewclimate.org
The Pew Center on Global Climate Change works to
    develop solutions to climate change.

United States Environmental Protection Agency (EPA)
Ariel Rios Building
1200 Pennsylvania Avenue NW
Washington, DC 20460
(202) 272-0167
Web site: http://www.epa.gov
The EPA is an organization of the United States govern-
    ment whose mission is to protect human health and
    environment. It has put extensive funding into research
    on climate change and how it affects our ecosystems
    and society.

United States Global Change Research Program (USGCRP)
1717 Pennsylvania Avenue NW, Suite 250
Washington, DC 20006
(202) 223-6262
Web site: http://www.globalchange.gov
Begun in 1989, the USGCRP coordinates and integrates
    federal research on changes in the global environment
    and their implications for society. The program engages

in a number of activities aimed at strengthening climate change research in the United States.

World Health Organization (WHO)
Avenue Appia 20
1211 Geneva 27
Switzerland
Tel.: 41-22-721-21-11
Web site: http://www.who.int/en
WHO is the directing and coordinating authority for health within the United Nations system. It is responsible for providing leadership on global health matters and pro-vides information on how the fundamental requirements for human health—including safe drinking water, suffi-cient food, and shelter—will be affected by rising sea levels due to climate change.

WEB SITES

Due to the changing nature of Internet links, Rosen Publishing has developed an online list of Web sites related to the sub-ject of this book. This site is updated regularly. Please use this link to access the list:

http://www.rosenlinks.com/sttr/sea

FOR FURTHER READing

Amsel, Sheri. *Everything Kids' Environment Book: Learn How You Can Help the Environment by Getting Involved at School, at Home, or at Play*. New York, NY: Adams Media, 2007.

Bradman, Tony. *Under the Weather: Stories About Climate Change*. London, England: Frances Lincoln Children's Books, 2010.

Hall, Julie, and Sarah Lane. *A Hot Planet Needs Cool Kids: Understanding Climate Change and What You Can Do About It*. Seattle, WA: Green Goat Books, 2007.

Johnson, Rebecca L. *Investigating Climate Change: Scientists' Search for Answers in a Warming World*. Breckenridge, CO: Twenty-First Century Books, 2008.

Kaye, Cathryn Berger. *Going Blue: A Teen Guide to Saving Our Oceans, Lakes, Rivers, & Wetlands*. Minneapolis, MN: Free Spirit Publishing, 2010.

Kaye, Cathryn Berger. *A Kids Guide to Climate Change and Global Warming: How to Take Action*. Minneapolis, MN: Free Spirit Publishing, 2009.

Koponen, Libby. *Floods* (True Books: Earth Science). San Francisco, CA: Children's Press, 2009.

Kusky, Timothy M. *Climate Change: Shifting Glaciers, Deserts, and Climate Belts*. New York, NY: Facts On File, 2008.

Ride, Sally, and Tam O'Shaughnessy. *Mission Planet Earth: Our World and Its Changing Climate*. New York, NY: Flash Point, 2009.

Woods, Michael, and Mary B. Woods. *Floods* (Disasters Up Close). Mankato, MN: Lerner, 2007.

BIBLIOGraphy

Agrawala, S., et al. *Development and Climate Change in Bangladesh: Focus on Coastal Flooding and the Sundarbans*. Paris, France: Organisation for Economic Co-operation and Development (OECD), 2003.

Centers for Ocean Sciences Education Excellence. "Ocean Systems." Retrieved September 2011 (http://cosee. umaine.edu/cfuser/resources/tr_sea_level.pdf).

Congressional Budget Office. *Potential Impacts of Climate Change in the United States*. Washington, DC: Congressional Budget Office, 2009.

Dudley, Robert W., and Martha G. Nielsen. *Inventory and Protection of Salt Marshes from Risks of Sea-Level Rise at Acadia National Park, Maine*. Reston, VA: U.S. Department of the Interior Geologic Survey, 2011.

EPA. "Science and Technology: Climate Change." Retrieved September 2011 (http://www.epa.gov/gateway/science/ climatechange.html).

Klein, Caroline. *Below Sea Level: Modern Architecture & Design in the Netherlands*. Lakewood, NJ: Innovative Logistics, 2011.

OECD. *Cities and Climate Change*. Paris, France: OECD Publishing, 2010.

Ward, Diane Raines. *Water Wars: Drought, Flood, Folly, and the Politics of Thirst*. New York, NY: Riverhead Books, 2002.

Ward, Peter Douglas. *The Flooded Earth: Our Future in a World Without Ice Caps*. New York, NY: Basic Books, 2010.

Ward, Peter Douglas. *Under a Green Sky: Global Warming, the Mass Extinctions of the Past, and What They Mean for Our Future*. New York, NY: Smithsonian Books, 2007.

Young, Rob, and Orrin H. Pilkey. *The Rising Sea*. Washington, DC: Island Press/Shearwater Books, 2009.

INDex

A

accommodation, as response to rising sea levels, 21, 23, 24, 25
  in Maine, 30
  in New York City, 37, 38
  through saltwater farming, 28–29
Antarctica, 12, 15, 20
architecture, and flood prevention/adaption, 39–41
Architecture for Disaster Relief, 41
Arctic, the, 15
Ark, 41

B

Bowman, Malcolm, 38

C

coastal environments, protecting, 51–53

D

Duxbury Beach Preservation group, 52

E

ecosystems, threats to fragile and threatened, 14–16, 51
energy
  reducing amount used, 47–51
  renewable sources of, 51

G

geoengineering, 42–44
glaciers, melting of, 9, 10–12, 34, 46

global warming, 5, 7, 26, 36, 41, 45, 46, 53
  and human activity, 9–10
  need to slow, 18, 19–20
  reversing effects of, 43
greenhouse gases, 10, 43, 44, 46, 47

H

Hodges, Carl, 28

I

ice sheets, melting of, 9, 10–12, 20, 34, 46
Irene, Hurricane 6–7

J

Jacob, Klaus, 37–38
Japan, flooding in, 13

M

Maasbommel Project, 39–41
Maine, strategies for flooding in, 30

N

Netherlands, and flood prevention, 32, 39–41
New York City
  response strategies for, 36–39
  threat to by flooding, 4–7, 36

P

protection, as response to rising sea levels, 21, 23, 24, 25

ABOUT THE AUTHOR

Susan Meyer is an author who lives in New York City, only a few blocks from a part of the city that is vulnerable to rising floodwaters. She is committed to reducing her carbon footprint by both not owning a car and unplugging cell phone chargers when not in use.

PHOTO CREDITS